formula one
THROUGH THE LENS

formula one
THROUGH THE LENS

FOUR DECADES OF MOTOR SPORT PHOTOGRAPHY BY
NIGEL SNOWDON
and DIANA BURNETT

Text and Layout: Steve Small

HAZLETON Publishing

formula one
THROUGH THE LENS
is published by
Hazleton Publishing Ltd
3 Richmond Hill
Richmond
Surrey TW10 6RE

Colour reproduction by
Vision Reprographics Ltd
Milton Keynes

Printed in England by
Butler & Tanner Ltd
Frome, Somerset

ISBN: 1-874557-18-7

distributors

UNITED KINGDOM
Biblios Ltd, Star Road
Partridge Green
West Sussex RH13 8LD
Tel: 01403 710971
Fax: 01403 711143

NORTH AMERICA
Motorbooks International
PO Box 1, 729 Prospect Ave., Osceola
Wisconsin 54020, USA
Tel: (1) 715 294 3345
Fax: (1) 715 294 4448

AUSTRALIA
Technical Book and Magazine Co. Pty
295 Swanston Street, Melbourne
Victoria 3000
Tel: (03) 9663 3951
Fax: (03) 9663 2094

NEW ZEALAND
David Bateman Ltd
PO Box 100-242
North Shore Mail Centre
Auckland 1330
Tel: (9) 415 7664
Fax: (9) 415 8892

SOUTH AFRICA
Motorbooks
341 Jan Smuts Avenue
Craighall Park, Johannesburg
Tel: (011) 325 4458/60
Fax: (011) 325 4146

contents

publisher
RICHARD POULTER

art editor
STEVE SMALL

managing editor
PETER LOVERING

production manager
STEVEN PALMER

publishing development manager
SIMON MAURICE

business development manager
SIMON SANDERSON

sales promotion
CLARE KRISTENSEN

Half-title page: Big lenses and fast reflexes are the order of the day at Silverstone in 1997, as the Tyrrell of Mika Salo flashes past.

Facing title page: The fog and rain hang over the Nürburgring circuit and an atmosphere of calm pervades the pits. Jochen Rindt sits quietly in his Brabham BT26-Repco during practice for the 1968 German Grand Prix.

Title verso page: Dutch Grand Prix, Zandvoort, 1966. Jack Brabham (16), Denny Hulme and Jim Clark all have their eyes on the starter, waiting for the flag to drop.

Opposite: Alan Jones flies in the Saudia Leyland Williams FW07C at the 1981 Dutch Grand Prix.

acknowledgements

I would like to thank David Phipps of Phipps Photographic, Peter Sachs of The Klemantaski Collection and Paul Vestey of GP Library for their kind permission to use those photographs of mine which are now in their collections.

N.S.

foreword by
Jackie Stewart OBE

Nigel Snowdon has been part of the Grand Prix circuit for as many years as I have been participating in Formula 1 as a driver and now as a team owner. His cheery face and his ever-ready lens are very much part of our scene in every corner of the world. Nigel is a true professional who one doesn't necessarily have to speak to every day to feel that you know him well.

What is produced in this book is an excellent record of his professional life. When I look through the photographs they bring back great memories, sad recollections, some chuckles and some laughter too. There are even some surprises – incidents that I had almost forgotten about and that had somehow or other nearly slipped away.

Long may Nigel Snowdon continue to tramp the circuits of the world. This mild, polite and well-mannered man has a sharp eye. He has known so many of the Formula 1 drivers throughout the years and, as is clear from this book, he is always ready to take a great photograph.

Jackie Stewart pictured in a happy family group with his wife Helen, grandson Dylan and son Paul, together with one of the Stewart Grand Prix team's cars.

introduction

nigel snowdon

grand prix
marathon man

Above: Reflections of the 'Swinging Sixties'. Resplendent in a natty hat, Nigel is framed by a racing car's rear-view mirror.

T was in 1963 that Nigel Snowdon, armed with his camera gear, a trackside pass and wide-eyed enthusiasm, first attended the British Grand Prix at Silverstone. Little did he realise that a new world was about to open up to him and that for most of the next 35 years his life would be consumed by a passion for motor racing photography.

Since that early foray, he has attended more than 450 World Championship Grands Prix, most of them in company with his wife Diana Burnett. Their photographs have been featured in countless magazines, books and newspapers around the globe, and this volume serves as a retrospective of their work.

Above: One of Nigel's early pictures from the Tasman series captures Jim Clark in happy mood as he chats with Jack Brabham and the late Geoff Sykes, who gave Nigel great help and encouragement in those early days.

After his summer sojourn in 1963, Nigel returned to his job in Sydney with Qantas, and continued to develop his photographic skills at his nearest tracks, Bathurst and Warwick Farm. He was fortunate that Geoff Sykes, another expat, was running the Warwick Farm circuit at the time. With his help and encouragement, the door was opened for Nigel to begin to establish himself on the motor racing scene. Crucial, at this time, was the opportunity to rub shoulders with the Grand Prix stars of the day in the Tasman series. Each winter the 'circus' arrived Down Under for a few weeks and thus fuelled Nigel's desire to join this exciting troupe and take part in their trips around the globe.

A brief return to Europe in 1966 took in the Monaco Grand Prix, and during the long sea voyage back to Australia Nigel resolved to return the following year to build a career as a motor sport photographer. On board ship, he was fortunate enough to meet Diana, then a teacher, who had been on a working trip to England. She too had the wanderlust and was keen to travel. Obviously their attraction was mutual for they arranged to meet in Hong Kong the following May and then travel on to Europe together to take in the Monaco Grand Prix. They have been together ever since. The trip was funded in part by the proceeds of Nigel's first book, entitled *The Ultimate Excitement*. It caused quite a stir when export copies were seized by unwitting Australian Customs officials who obviously thought its contents were of an entirely different nature!

Having settled in England, Nigel and Diana took various temporary positions to make ends meet. Nigel opted for shift work as an ambulance driver and Diana returned to teaching, before moving to a photographic studio where she was responsible for the accounts. This provided a valuable grounding for the running of their own business, Snowdon and Associates, which they set up in 1978.

Nigel quickly proved his talent and in 1968 joined the David Phipps Photographic Agency to become a fully fledged member of the Grand Prix scene. In the thirty years since then he has travelled the world many times over, and, between them, Nigel and Diana have missed only a fraction of the Grands Prix that have been held. They have also attended scores of other motor sport events encompassing sports car and GT racing, touring cars, Indy car racing and rallying.

Outwardly it seems a glamorous lifestyle, but in reality it is an extremely demanding one. The hectic travel schedules, coupled with ever-shrinking deadlines for delivery, leave little time during the season for relaxation. The Grand Prix world is a fast-moving one, which sees people come and go with ever-increasing regularity. To have been on the scene for such a long period of time has demanded huge reserves of stamina, endless patience and unending enthusiasm, and these are attributes which have stood the Snowdons in good stead during their long tenure in Formula 1. I have worked with both Nigel and Diana for more than a decade and it has been a pleasure to help put together this book with them.

Nigel, who has used Nikon cameras since the start of his photographic career and has always enjoyed a close working relationship with the company, was particularly keen that his work should be represented by his black and white photography. This is not to decry colour, but the creation of the black and white print is an art in itself and the quality of this workmanship can be enjoyed in this volume.

Between us, we have endured the painful process of pruning down a massive number of images. At first it was with gentle sadness that shots were left to one side, but this soon gave way to what seemed like heartless brutality as long-favoured photographs were forced to join the discard pile! What remains is a distillation of nearly four decades of wonderful motor racing images. Hopefully, they elicit some of the excitement, pain, fun, drama, triumph and tragedy that is motor racing.

Steve Small,
Windsor,
Berkshire
1998

Above: This was how close you could sometimes get to the action in the Seventies. Nigel's shot of François Cevert in the Tyrrell at Zandvoort also includes his wife Diana Burnett to the left of the frame.

Below: Two of Grand Prix racing's longest-serving photographers: Nigel with Akira Mase, photographed in 1997. *Photo courtesy of Bryn Williams*

chapter 1
circuits

Close to the action. Just a low concrete-block wall separates photographers from the machines at Silverstone's Copse Corner in 1963 as Graham Hill drifts by in his BRM, chased by the Ferrari of John Surtees.

'We were so close to the cars that a 35 mm or 50 mm lens would be sufficient to fill the frame with the car, but now, some thirty yards back from the apex, a 600 mm lens is the order of the day and a side-on pan shot is the only picture you can take.'

classic circuits
spa-francorchamps

'I loved the old Spa. It had a magic about it; seemingly everywhere you went on the circuit there was the opportunity to make really great pictures. The new circuit, though less daunting, still manages to evoke the spirit of the old and puts to shame many of the modern purpose-built tracks, which are pretty faceless.'

Top: Looking out over the valley from the vantage point above Rivage towards Pouhon on the new part of the circuit. 'You are among the crowd, and this is a great viewing place for spectators.'

Right: La Source. 'It's a slow corner but very tricky and a good place for drivers to overtake. The restaurant on the right is now the F1 Paddock Club, but I remember it well during my visits for the 24-hour sports car race. It was a rare chance to have a beer and take a few photos as well!'

Opposite: Eau Rouge, one of the most exciting corners in Formula 1. 'You've really got to be so brave here.' The sparks always flew at this point on the circuit in the turbo era: Piquet in the Williams-Honda leads Alboreto, Prost, Berger and the rest of the field in the 1987 race.

CIRCUITS

classic circuits
monte carlo

'I first went to Monaco in 1965, and it was very different then, despite the fact that the track itself has changed little. It's unreal to look at the top photo and see a photographer standing completely unprotected as Jack Brabham and Jackie Stewart race down from Mirabeau towards the Station Hairpin. I once had a narrow escape when Pedro Rodriguez stuffed his BRM into a wall at the spot where I had been walking by only seconds earlier.'

Right: The first time Bruce McLaren ran his own F1 car, painted white especially for the film *Grand Prix.* 'A photographer could walk right round the track.' Note the complete lack of Armco and the dangerous-looking sign post.

Opposite top: The swimming pool section made a great shot as this 1973 picture of Jackie Stewart in the Tyrrell leading Emerson Fittipaldi's Lotus shows. 'Unfortunately now it has become polluted with all sorts of visual diarrhoea with advertising hoardings and a bridge across the track.'

Opposite bottom: Another classic shot from 1982 as eventual winner Riccardo Patrese in the Brabham leads the cars in single file down past the Tip Top bar on the right. 'This was a place where drivers such as Graham Hill and Denny Hulme and their mechanics came for post-race celebrations in more social times. People used to sit on the Armco on both sides of the road and watch the exotic cars such as Lamborghinis cruise by. We don't frequent it any more as not only has the price of the beer spiralled out of sight, but Diana and I, along with the rest of the F1 media, are likely to be heading for Nice airport straight after the race to catch the earliest flight possible back home to try and meet ever more demanding press schedules.'

classic circuits
monza

'I didn't use to like going to Monza, but I do now. Unlike a lot of other places, it's become easier to work, but the race is so short that you only have time to shoot close to the start-finish if you want to get to the podium for the presentation.

'This shot is from the FIAT Tower looking down towards the Goodyear chicane in the 1983 race. I used to get permission to do the start from here and it shows two quintessential elements of Monza: the old and long-since disused banked part of the circuit on the right, evoking memories of legendary cars and drivers from the past, and the ever-changing graffiti on the track, which, despite the misspelling, remembers Ronnie Peterson, who so tragically lost his life here after an accident in 1978.'

circuits lost
nürburgring

'I always used to spend one practice session at least out at the Karussell. I have been driven through this banked corner and it was the most incredible feeling: you are just pressed down into the car.' Ronnie Peterson *(left)* driving a March is about to enter the 180-degree turn in 1976. This was the last time the German Grand Prix was held on the full Nordschleife track which ran for some 14.167 miles through the Eifel Mountains due to the horrendous accident which befell Niki Lauda.

Below: Just a year earlier and under sunny skies, this is the classic start shot at the South Curve. 'The cars used to disappear and you would have a wait of about seven minutes before the leader came past again. It was possible for photographers to cross the track in those days and with only 14 laps in the race the rush was on to find another spot in order to get a different type of race shot.' Heading the crocodile is Niki Lauda's Ferrari with the Brabham of Carlos Pace in pursuit. Behind are Depailler (Tyrrell), Mass (McLaren), the eventual winner Reutemann (Brabham), Stuck (March), Regazzoni (Ferrari), Emerson Fittipaldi (McLaren) and the rest of the field.

circuits lost
clermont-ferrand • paul ricard • dijon

The French Grand Prix has been held at many venues during its long existence. Inevitably some hold more cherished memories than others. Clermont-Ferrand *(above left)*, high in the Auvergne, was a magnificent test of driver and machine, but the facilities were primitive with the paddock nothing more than a sloping field. This is the start of the 1970 race with Jacky Ickx in the Ferrari leading Beltoise (Matra, 21) and Amon (March, 14).

Left: A complete opposite in terms of facilities and topography was the Paul Ricard circuit near Toulon. Flat, hot and dusty, it was dominated by the daunting mile-long Mistral Straight but was seen as a very safe venue until the death of Elio de Angelis in a testing accident in 1986. 'The Mistral was then emasculated and both literally and metaphorically it wasn't half the circuit it had been.' The photo shows the crowd gathered in the pit lane to greet the 1982 winner René Arnoux as he takes the chequered flag in his Renault. There was a bit of a to-do here, as he had reneged on a pre-race agreement to let team-mate Prost win and bolster his championship bid.

Above: Dijon 1979. 'I never really liked Dijon as a circuit; I could never make really nice pictures there, so I was quite glad that they didn't hold a Grand Prix there too often!' This was one idea which worked quite well: filling the picture with plenty of sky to show Jabouille's Renault disappearing over the brow.

'The Zandvoort circuit was really super, a great place to work and play. The beach-resort hotels were close by serving excellent food, and an easy-going atmosphere always made it a great race meeting to attend.'

'The picture on the right is one of our best-selling works, especially in colour. The composition of the cars, with Alan Jones leading the way in his Williams, is good and there's not a lot of contentious advertising. In fact it's really a generic picture that says "Grand Prix racing". Even though it's nearly twenty years old, it still goes on selling as a stock shot. Good grief! If Jonesey reads this he'll be after commission!'

Below: This view gives an impression of the sweeping curves set amid the sand dunes. You could stand right on the corner and get close-ups of the drivers at work or moody wide angles such as this, when the clouds and the ambience take precedence over the car.

circuits lost
zandvoort

Racing in Barcelona in the Nineties means a visit to the Catalunya circuit, a modern, rather featureless and antiseptic track with little or no atmosphere. However, in the late Sixties and early Seventies the race was held on the Montjuich circuit situated in a public park in the centre of the city.

Scenery *à la* Monte Carlo and hot, sunny weather all helped make dramatic photos like this shot from 1969. Jack Brabham and Jackie Stewart do battle but the high wings on struts were about to have their last hurrah. Jochen Rindt and Graham Hill both escaped relatively unscathed from major shunts when their aerofoils collapsed during the race and the outlandish devices were mercifully banned before they could endanger driver safety again.

Below right: Splendid architecture provides a marvellous backdrop as Jackie Stewart and his Tyrrell-Ford speed past on their way to victory in 1971.

circuits lost
montjuich park

circuits lost

österreichring

The original Österreichring was built in 1969 but it seemed to hark back to an earlier era more in tune with classic mountain circuits such as the Nürburgring and Spa. Its fast, sweeping curves set in dramatic scenery are clearly shown in both of Nigel's photos here.

In the pouring rain you could make dramatic pictures like the one on the right taken in 1975 from a vantage point up in the crowd. Lauda, Hunt, Depailler and Fittipaldi head towards the daunting Bosch Kurve. 'Not a place for the faint-hearted.'

Below: A feast for both the eyes and the ears as the Styrian Mountains reverberate to the glorious sound of the Matra V12 propelling Jacques Laffite and his Ligier to victory in the 1981 race.

After a race each for Sebring and Riverside, Watkins Glen became the home of the US Grand Prix in 1961 and for two decades was the Formula 1 teams' traditional Stateside venue in the 'fall'. The circuit was infamous for its 'Bog' and the natives thereof, who could easily take umbrage without the slightest provocation. No doubt under the influence of alcohol or more exotic substances, they would pick out a car – or even, legend has it, a Greyhound bus – to trash and burn out. Was this a 'happening'? The photo *(left)* could be a scene from Woodstock.

Below: Ronnie Peterson leads the way in his Lotus followed by Reutemann, Hunt, Fittipaldi, Hailwood, Hulme and Scheckter in 1973. However, the weekend was overshadowed by the death of François Cevert in practice.

circuits lost
watkins glen

If truth be told, Shoreline Drive apart, Long Beach is a bit of a dump, being the port for Los Angeles to the north. Nevertheless it became an extremely popular venue for Formula 1 in the mid-Seventies, and is remembered affectionately by many who attended the races. The permanently moored *Queen Mary* not only provided an imposing skyline but was also the lavish setting for generous hospitality provided by corporate sponsors.

While the Glen was geographically somewhat remote, Long Beach was right on the doorstep of a huge conurbation, and thus pulled in hordes of intrigued spectators, many of whom were unfamiliar with the world of Grand Prix racing and its intricacies. Chris Pook, whose brainchild the street circuit was, eventually found it prohibitively expensive to stage F1 round the houses and took his ball to play with the guys from CART.

Both these shots feature Niki Lauda. *Left:* The Austrian guides his McLaren through the temporary course in 1983 with the *Queen Mary* looming in the background, while at the inaugural F1 race seven years earlier *(below)* his Ferrari is dwarfed like some slot-racing car by the towering office building behind.

circuits lost
long beach

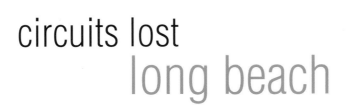

Three more US tracks which hosted Grands Prix in the Eighties.

'Detroit always made for interesting pictures, with many buildings and underpasses, strong light and shade. There was always something to shoot behind the car.'

Far left: A Detroit practice shot from 1983 featuring Michele Alboreto (the race winner) in his Tyrrell followed by Marc Surer in the Arrows. They were the leading Cosworth runners at this race, battling to stay in touch with the more powerful turbos of the time. Tight street circuits offered the normally aspirated cars a rare chance to shine.

Below left: Spectators got a great uninterrupted view of the action at the Las Vegas track, the most artificial of all the circuits seen in modern-day Formula 1.
'We would walk through Caesars Palace on the way to practice and stop off to put a few dollars in the slot machines. I like the heat, so working here in Nevada was no problem for me. Nobody thought much of the "Mickey Mouse" circuit laid out in the Caesars Palace car park, but it really wasn't too bad at all for photos.'

Below: Dallas, aka Concrete Alley. 'The cars just used to disappear into these seemingly blind canyons of wire fencing. I always remember a lap or so before the end of the race, photographers were busy with cutters snipping away sections of the fencing. Large holes would appear to allow them to get a decent finish shot.'

circuits lost
detroit
las vegas
dallas

the southern hemisphere
kyalami
rio de janeiro
adelaide

Above left: 'Kyalami was brilliant in the old days. It was a very old-fashioned circuit by European standards, but fast and exciting. When we went back in 1992 it had changed quite a bit and had the modern problem of cars being unable to overtake one another. The track was now also lined by corporate boxes and its atmosphere had changed, as had nearby Johannesburg, which wasn't a particularly pleasant place to visit.'

Left: The huge grandstand towers over the main straight of Rio de Janeiro's Jacarepaguá circuit (now the Autodromo Nelson Piquet), which played host to the Brazilian Grand Prix in the 1980s. 'The weather was invariably hot and very humid and the fans in the grandstands used to be hosed with water from the fire tenders during race morning to help cool them down. I used to like this circuit because after the practice sessions you could get to the beach in about 20 minutes. One downside to working at this track, which was built on marshland, was the chance that you would encounter a snake in the infield.'

Above: Adelaide in 1987 with Nelson Piquet leading Alain Prost as they pass the Stag Hotel. 'This was a favourite place for everybody. It was the last race in the season and there was a great end-of-term atmosphere. I was sorry that the Grand Prix moved to Melbourne, because they have so much in the Australian sporting calendar already – what with the horse racing, the tennis, the golf etc. – but money talks.'

brands hatch

Right: 'When I first came back to England, Brands Hatch was the first track I visited. I was knocked out by it then and I still love working there today, but sadly no longer shooting Formula 1 as it's now far too dangerous for Grands Prix. It has always been one of my favourite circuits, because its undulating nature offers a fabulous view and great photo opportunities. The air displays *(right)* were always part and parcel of the Grand Prix weekend. One year a Harrier jump-jet blew down most of the hospitality area in the paddock during a demonstration!'

Below: The start of the 1964 British Grand Prix as the pack pour into Paddock Bend. Jim Clark's Lotus *(left),* Graham Hill's BRM *(centre)* and Dan Gurney's Brabham *(right)* are in control. Giving immediate chase are John Surtees in the Ferrari *(extreme right)* and Denny Hulme's Brabham, which partly masks Bruce McLaren scrabbling along the grass in his Cooper.

chapter 2
fans

Monza 1986 and the *tifosi* surge forward as the gates are opened to let the crowd invade the track at the finish. 'Somewhere in the scrum are a couple of guys on mopeds who were overwhelmed. The police had given up trying to control the situation after wading in with their batons. It was just madness and I stood their laughing while photographing it!'

Left: 'Mansell mania at Silverstone was a phenomenon. It hasn't been like that since, not even for Damon Hill. The tabloid press were instrumental in bringing people to see a Grand Prix who previously had no interest in motor racing. They came just to support Mansell. I never thought the British would show such emotion, but the crowds at Silverstone in the early Nineties were passionate and fanatical like a soccer crowd. And I have to say I've never much liked football.'

Argentina: 'When Carlos Reutemann came past the stands the fans would go wild, cheering and throwing paper into the air. If a Brazilian such as Fittipaldi or Pace came past the response was not quite so enthusiastic . . .'

Right: Le Mans. 'This is one of my favourite pictures. I was in the pits and looking for something to photograph when I saw this plaque across the track. It marks the spot where 82 people died when a car careered into the crowd back in 1955. These fans are waiting for the finish and it shows. A Ferrari 512S flashes past, but a look at virtually everybody in the photo will show the tiredness that nearly 24 hours of motor racing brings on. And they aren't even working!'

† 11 Juin 1955

Top: These three fans in Austria had the best seats in the (tree) house. 'Some of these structures were amazing, they had portable TVs, radios, provisions, everything to make watching the race as comfortable as possible.'

Above right: Imola, early on race day down at Tosa. Pasta, pasta everywhere. 'The smell of the cooking was incredible, it is one of the things that give the San Marino Grand Prix such atmosphere.'

Right: Monza 1996 with Rubens Barrichello signing autographs at the gates to the paddock. The fans would scream and wave the moment a driver appeared, and most would take the time to sign as many autographs as they could. Such was the bedlam that now the *tifosi* are kept away from the paddock completely. 'It's so sad, it really is. It's the way Formula 1 is going nowadays: all very sanitary, very impersonal . . .'

FANS

Left: Human termites seem to be devouring this Agip hoarding at Monza, a practice no longer tolerated. 'By the end of race day the sign was completely in tatters. If you walked past there, you were likely to be hit on the head with a salami roll or an empty Coke can.'

Below: Dressed for a thrill. These Michael Schumacher fans are the centre of attention and they know it, posing for photographers in their lovingly assembled attire.

Bottom: Rosie's Bar at Monaco. 'You could always be assured of a really warm welcome from Rosie. She would say, "I saw your pictures of the bar in *Autocourse*. Have a drink with us, Nigel." In practice the public weren't allowed into the area where Rosie's bar stood, but as photographers we had access, so we could grab a snack in between sessions.'

FANS

Above: Italian Grand Prix, Monza, 1983. Nelson Piquet (Brabham) and Eddie Cheever (Renault) have taken the chequered flag in first and third places respectively but now they have the task of getting themselves and their cars back to *parc fermé* in one piece. 'They rush out onto the circuit and woe betide anyone who stops his car as it is likely to be stripped in seconds. Note the guy doing a somersault in the background.'

Right: A standing ovation for Jody. The defining moment of the 1974 British Grand Prix at Brands Hatch. Spectators in the Paddock Hill grandstand rise as one when Scheckter in the Tyrrell overtakes Lauda's Ferrari to snatch the lead, and ultimate victory. 'This shot was taken with a 500 mm lens, and the excitement of the fans provides more action than the cars doing battle.'

FANS

chapter 3
drivers

Ayrton Senna caught in a relaxed moment.
'I really like this portrait; he just came to the
edge of the pit garage and all I could see of
him was this profile as he looked out over the
pit lane. Quite a number of people have bought
original prints of this shot, so I guess it
captures Ayrton in a way that his fans would
like to remember him.'

bruce mclaren

jack brabham

denny hulme

'When I first started motor racing photography I was living in Australia and I have to admit that Jack Brabham was my hero. I was very new on the scene and, despite being a double World Champion, he was a very approachable person. You could always talk to him, though he was a man of few words – and even more so nowadays as all those years of racing with an engine right behind his head have taken their toll on his hearing.'

'Bruce McLaren was another driver I admired and not just because he gave me my first commission as a motor racing photographer. He was involved in the development of the Lola sports car and I did some pictures of him at Goodwood. After that, I took lots of photos at the original factory in the days before he started building his own F1 car.'

'Denny was a real character and a genuine guy. Nicknamed "The Bear", he sometimes had an up-and-down relationship with the motor racing press but underneath that tough exterior he was kind of a shy person. He always used to see where you were shooting out on the circuit and would often come over after practice and ask, "Why were you shooting from such and such a place?" '

'What can you say about Innes? I didn't know him terribly well when he was racing, but I did when he came back into the sport a few years later as a journalist with *Autocar* and *Road and Track*. He was the most incredible character. After dinner one night in Brazil he said, "You'll join me for a wee dram, won't you?" The night-cap was the best part of a bottle of scotch, and though I had a hangover the next morning he seemed totally unaffected by it. A lovely man.'

'I admired both Siffert and Rodriguez for their prowess in sports cars. They were quite brilliant in Porsche 917s, which were extremely difficult cars to drive. Siffert was a very pleasant and genuine man. I remember he was so emotional after he had won the British Grand Prix for Rob Walker at Brands Hatch in 1968. Everyone was so thrilled for both of them, it was a real fairytale story. Pedro had a wicked smile and a good sense of humour. He cut a strange figure, a Mexican wearing a deer-stalker hat. Rodriguez obviously enjoyed the life of a racing driver, he would race anything anywhere, which in the end cost him his life . . .'

innes ireland

pedro rodriguez

jo siffert

graham hill

jim clark

'Graham was a ladies' man, a wonderful after-dinner speaker, the epitome of a racing driver in those days. He knew what he wanted and he could also be quite sharp and certainly didn't suffer fools gladly. But he became much more amenable and talkative once he started his own team later on, especially after he packed in driving. He was an extremely witty person and a great ambassador for the sport.'

'I first met Jim Clark when he was "Down Under" for the Tasman series in Australia and New Zealand and found him to be quite an unassuming man and a very nice person. He was interested in photography and showed me some of the pictures he had taken. A truly great driver: very, very quick indeed. He was one of my all-time favourites.'

'I've watched Jackie almost from the time he first came into motor racing. I remember him in Ken Tyrrell's Formula 3 Cooper, and he's never changed in all this time. Without doubt, Jackie was always a very talented driver and possessed a shrewd brain, which has seen him succeed in many areas since he retired from driving in 1973. It's nice to have him back on the scene as a team owner with his son Paul.

'Diana and I were once shooting the horse trials at Badminton, and she got some pictures of Princess Anne falling from her horse into the water. Jackie asked if he could have some prints to give to her and we were delighted to oblige. It also gave us the chance to put on the back "photography by Snowdon"!'

'Jochen Rindt was very easy to photograph, a very good subject. Unlike some drivers, he would never turn away or pick his nose or do something to spoil the shot, but as a person I found him rather cold and arrogant.'

jackie stewart

jochen rindt

emerson fittipaldi

mario andretti

'Mario was like Graham Hill in that they were true champion drivers who could get into any car and drive really well. I photographed Mario in Grand Prix cars, sports cars and Indy cars and he shone in all of those disciplines. Racing has been good to him and he has put a lot back into the sport. He's a great ambassador for motor racing worldwide, not just Formula 1.'

'You could probably say the same thing about Emerson, now he's reached the end of his driving career. He was very young and very shy at first, but he was coached by Colin Chapman and soon began to come out of his shell. Like all great drivers, there was something about him that made you think, "This guy's special," and he certainly was. It's a shame he saddled himself with his uncompetitive team in the second half of the Seventies – he largely wasted half his Formula 1 career.'

'Ronnie was probably my favourite driver of all. I was driven round several circuits by him in saloon cars and it was pretty special. He was always willing to try his hand at other sports such as golf and tennis, which was sometimes hilarious to watch. I once saw him bend a golf club around a tree at Watkins Glen when attempting a shot. He was a very quiet person. If you didn't know him, you could have to work very hard. The picture on the right was taken in 1978 at Monza on the day of his accident. When he saw me he just put on a big smile and I got some lovely shots. They were published in a Swedish magazine, and Ronnie's father wrote and asked if they could have some originals, he liked them so much . . .'

ronnie peterson

DRIVERS

peter revson

'I photographed Peter Revson quite a lot, as I worked for Yardley and Citibank. He was a typical American sportsman, very easy and pleasant. Much like their golfers and tennis players, Peter was aware of the value of sponsorship, and so if I asked him to do something for a picture he'd just do it.

'Before a testing session at Kyalami in 1974 he was asking my advice on buying a camera for his then girlfriend, Miss World, Marji Wallace. Minutes later his Shadow car was a heap of mangled wreckage and racing had claimed another victim.'

'Pace I didn't know very well, but Di did some lovely portraits of him and thought he was charming. It seems a cruel irony that he should have lost his life in a light-aircraft crash.'

'Mike was a very popular figure in the paddock. He was a genuine, open guy, full of life and great fun. It can't have been easy for him to build a new career on four wheels after achieving so much success on bikes, but he was a real racer, down to earth and totally without pretensions.'

carlos pace

mike hailwood

DRIVERS

carlos reutemann

niki lauda

james hunt

'Lauda always was an incredibly talented person and he always knew what he wanted – and usually he got it. In this picture he looks straight at you and even after his accident he would look straight into the camera as if to say, "Go on, I dare you, take a picture." His dedication was unreal, you've got to admire the guy.'

'Carlos Reutemann always seemed a moody sort of person. There were days when he was in a good mood and his disposition was sunny, as in the photo above, but on other days he would turn his head and not be happy at all to be photographed. I was an Alan Jones fan, so perhaps not as well disposed towards Carlos when they were together at Williams.'

'James made an early impression on me when I saw him leap out of his F3 car after a last-corner crash to punch Dave Morgan! He was a very unconventional guy, turning up to catch a plane dressed in a pair of shorts and T-shirt but no shoes. He didn't care at all about formality; he'd happily arrive at a sponsor's do very little better dressed on occasion. He always used to say what he thought, had a very good sense of humour and was a terrific squash player. I'd love to have played him . . .'

gilles villeneuve

alan jones

jody scheckter

'Villeneuve was a very spectacular driver and a real crowd-pleaser. He was always on the edge with his car but I'm afraid he wasn't one of my favourites. I never rated him with the top echelon like Clark, Stewart or Senna.'

'We knew Alan when he first came from Oz to race in Formula 3 and always liked him as a person – probably because he said what he thought and got stuck in. What he did in his early years with Williams was fantastic; Frank and Patrick Head owe him a lot.
  'He used to get into lots of different business ventures which came and went and always used to say, "You must come for a drink." The trouble was that he would never tell you where he was going to be!'

'From the time he bounced off the wall at Silverstone I always had a soft spot for Jody. He was a bit shy and extremely polite. He was a tremendous driver but once he left motor racing he just walked away and did his own thing. Now his sons are racing and we see him around on occasion. He hasn't changed much at all, he's still a really nice bloke.'

patrick depailler

jacques laffite

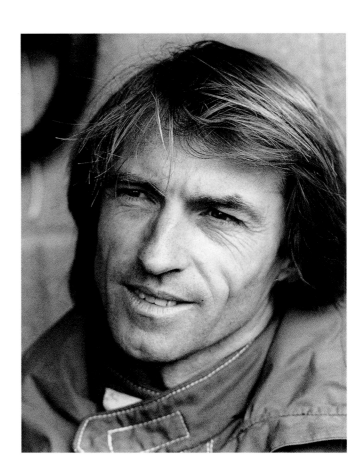

A trio of French drivers who all made it to the top of the ladder.

'I always admired Depailler's determination. His win at Monaco in 1978 was long overdue and everybody in the paddock was genuinely pleased for him. The way he came back after his hang-gliding accident to take on the challenge with Alfa Romeo showed what a gutsy little competitor he was.'

'Jacques was *the* joker of Formula 1; what a tremendous sense of humour. He once turned up to an early practice session at Dallas in his pyjamas and carrying a tooth brush as a light-hearted protest at the unearthly hour the cars were expected to take the track. Some of his golfing escapades are legendary as well. I've photographed him hitting his ball out from up in a tree.
    'But let's not forget he was a really good driver, his win in appalling weather conditions at Montreal in 1981 was quite brilliant. It was a real shame that the pile-up at Brands Hatch ended his F1 career prematurely. Luckily, he and his sense of humour are still regularly to be found in the paddock.'

'Arnoux was a strange little chap, scurrying around the paddock with his eyes forever darting about. He used to rush into the Elf motorhome – overalls half off and tied round his waist – and grab a roll or something and then be off, munching as he went, visiting somewhere else. In recent years he always seems to be around the paddock talking to everyone but I never knew what he did until I was told he works as a commentator for Rai Uno, the Italian TV channel.'

rené arnoux

riccardo patrese

keke rosberg

patrick tambay

'Riccardo was a real gentleman. When he first started he was seen as wild and dangerous, but he was really a quiet, sensitive man. He had an aura about him and as he matured he became one of the most popular guys around.'

'I never got too close to Keke because of the amount of cigarette smoke between me and him. He never seemed to be without a fag on the go. As soon as his car pulled into the pit a mechanic would hand him a cigarette.'

'Known as "Prince Charming", Patrick Tambay was always well groomed and very polite – an easy subject to photograph. Given a decent car he drove reasonably well, but I found him a bit bland compared to some of the other drivers of his era.'

nelson piquet

alain prost

nigel mansell

'Alain was always a bit special. Right from his early races for McLaren in 1980 Di said, "You must take pictures of him, he's a future World Champion."

'Forever chewing his nails, Prost was a great thinker; he must have learnt a lot from Lauda when they were together. He'd plan everything meticulously from his car preparation and race strategy to his business dealings with people. Today he runs his own team and they are one of the friendliest in the pit lane.'

'Piquet was a one-off. I remember he'd tell you anything you wanted to hear whether it was true or not. I liked him because of his mischievous sense of humour. How he managed to look after his string of lovely ladies and his offspring is a mystery!

'Once in Argentina he nearly ran me down. Apparently he'd been told to lose the car out on the circuit because it was illegal and he did just that, coming across the grass straight at me. He missed me and my camera bag by about a foot and a half. He got out of the car without looking back and walked straight back to the pits to tell Gordon Murray he thought he'd run down a photographer. When I came into the pit later on he said, "I thought I'd killed you." We were both pretty shaken up.'

'I think Mansell was one of the greatest, but he seemed to dramatise everything. He should have won an Oscar for some of his theatrics. But on the track he was just sensational. I remember him going around the outside of Berger in Mexico. It was unreal. Also in his dices with Senna – no way was Nigel going to give best.

'I think it's a shame that he didn't pack it in at the end of 1994, while he was still at the top.'

gerhard berger

jean alesi

ayrton senna

'I think Berger is the last character of the present era. At the circuits nowadays the current drivers are all becoming very bland, controlled by excessive PR. With Gerhard around he was always likely to puncture the pomposity of it all. He was unlucky to be racing against some great drivers like Prost, Piquet, Senna and Mansell, otherwise he might easily have been a champion himself.'

'It was wonderful to see Jean Alesi winning in Canada because I can't see him winning another Grand Prix, to be honest. He is blessed with so much driving talent but has, it seems, failed to develop the mentality required to succeed on a consistent basis. If he had not torn up his option to join Williams in 1991 and gone to Ferrari, who knows what he might have achieved?'

'Without doubt Senna was one of the finest drivers of all time. He was one of the greatest I've ever had the privilege to see. If you could talk to him about interests other than motor racing, such as model aircraft or sailing or children, he would be easy and relaxed, even chatty.
  'Ayrton was a complex individual. Obviously a man of enormous intelligence, he was also very sensitive. Despite his superstar status, he was, deep down, quite a shy and vulnerable person. A terrible loss to the sport. Irreplaceable.'

jacques villeneuve

damon hill

michael schumacher

'I think Villeneuve is a very shrewd customer. His grunge look and couldn't-care-less approach mask a calculating brain, a huge amount of driving talent and a burning desire to win. He has taken on Schumacher head to head and beaten him. That says it all.'

'A good family man, Damon has worked hard for all the success he has achieved and he is a credit to the sport. Give him a good car and he'll shine. He was great in his time at Williams, winning 21 races, but in the Arrows (with the exception of his drive in Hungary) some of his performances were very disappointing. It will be interesting to see if he can be a winner again now he has moved on to Jordan.'

'I put Schumacher on a par with Senna. I think he's absolutely brilliant, I really do. Leaving Benetton at the top to go to Ferrari and bringing them up to a point where winning the championship is a realistic proposition is a feat probably only he could have achieved. He's the complete professional and despite his lapse at Jerez I think he's still as popular as ever.'

chapter 4
ready for action

With the preliminaries complete, conversations in the paddock and pit garage are wound up and the time comes for the drivers to don their helmets and take to their working environment, the cockpit.

Over the next few pages, Nigel's photos portray the apprehension, concentration, stress, relaxation and even boredom experienced by the drivers before the action begins and they take to the track.

Above: Jack Brabham – mildly apprehensive? 1963

Above: Jim Clark – vociferous, 1966

Above right: John Surtees – impassive, 1967

Right: Jackie Stewart – inquisitive, 1968

READY FOR ACTION

READY FOR ACTION

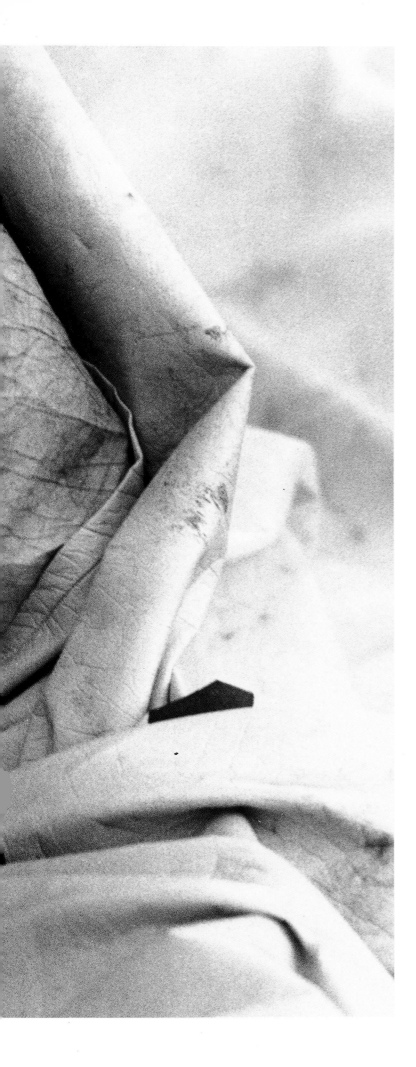

Above: René Arnoux – startled, 1983

Left: Ronnie Peterson – bored, 1974

Above: Alan Jones – activated, 1981

Right: Ayrton Senna – total concentration, 1991

READY FOR ACTION

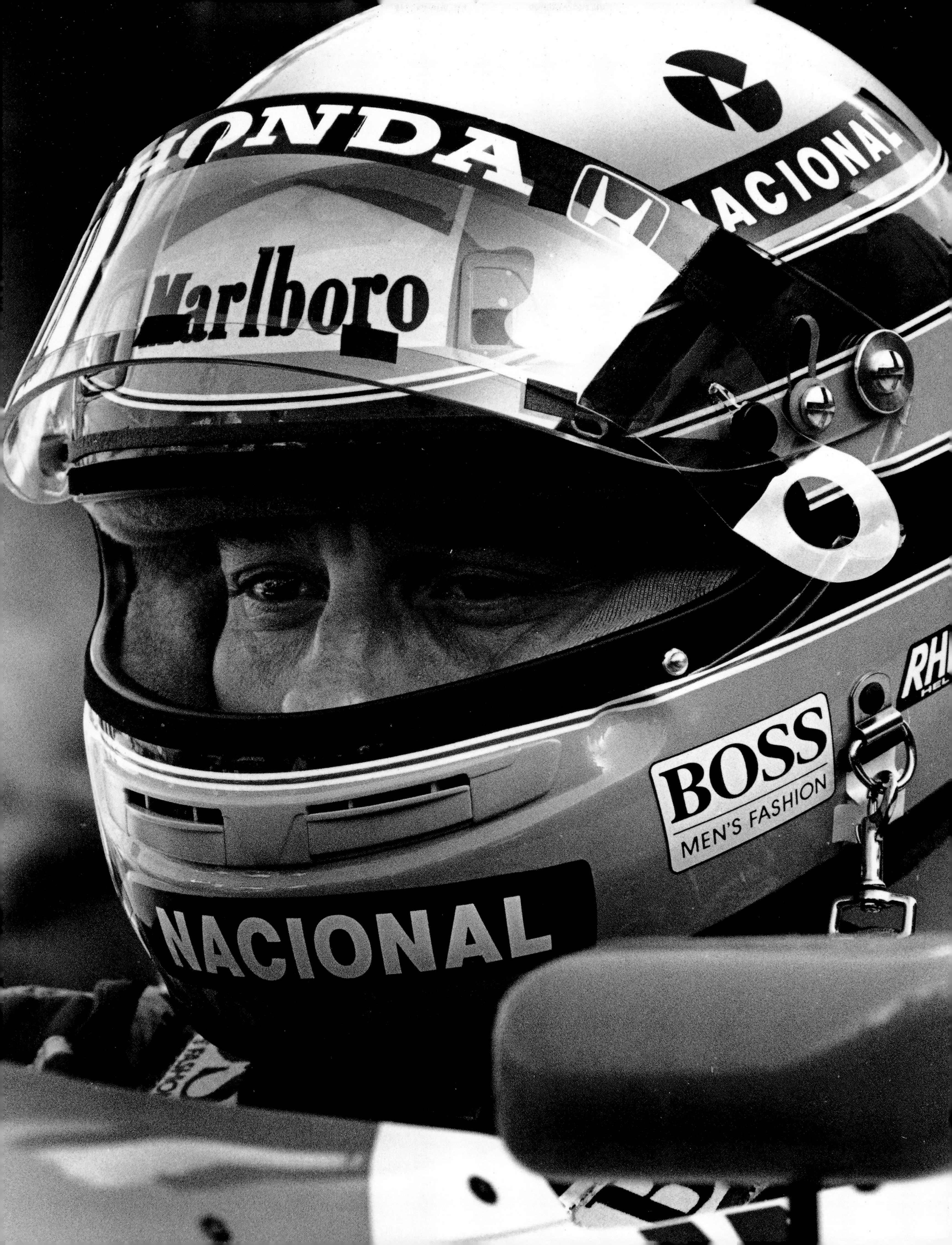
HONDA
NACIONAL
Marlboro
BOSS
MEN'S FASHION
NACIONAL

Above: Jean Alesi – languid, 1994

Above left: Nelson Piquet – in command, 1990

Left: Michael Schumacher – completely focused, 1996

READY FOR ACTION

Keke Rosberg – wishful thinker, 1983

READY FOR ACTION

action

Nigel has attended well over 450 World Championship races as well as many F1 non-championship events, although the latter sadly no longer appear in the racing calendar.

Here is just a tiny selection of the thousands of action shots he has taken. They represent a mini-history of Grand Prix racing spanning most of the last four decades.

Above: British Grand Prix, Silverstone, 1963. Perfect symmetry as John Surtees (Ferrari) and Graham Hill (BRM) chase Jack Brabham (Brabham) through Copse Corner. 'It was a real privilege to be allowed to go out and work just three feet from the action.'

Belgian Grand Prix, Spa-Francorchamps, 1963. 'These days all you can see is the eyes, you can't see anything else. In these shots taken from the inside of La Source you can really see the driver at work.'

Clockwise from left: Bruce McLaren (Cooper), Jim Clark (Lotus) and John Surtees (Ferrari) find their own particular line through the hairpin corner. Note the lack of a safety harness over the shoulders and roll-over bars that do not even come above the line of the drivers' helmets.

Above left: Dutch Grand Prix, Zandvoort, 1966. A trace of a smile from Jack Brabham as he cruises to victory in his Brabham-Repco. This was the first year of the new 3-litre formula and Jack's uncomplicated and reliable car was just what was required to take him to his third World Championship.

Left: British Grand Prix, Silverstone, 1967. Honda had chosen a much more technically advanced path in their early attempts to conquer Formula 1. John Surtees gave it his best shot, but ultimately failed. While the Brabham was nimble and forgiving, the Honda was too heavy and didn't handle well, negating any advantages the powerful V12 engine may have offered.

'These drivers were among the best in the world, the best of the day, so I always felt safe. Just watching these guys drifting past you was something else. Mind you, I wouldn't dream of standing as close in Formula 3. Too risky! It wasn't worth even the slim chance of getting hurt taking an F3 picture.'

ACTION

Above: German Grand Prix, Nürburgring, 1968.
Jacky Ickx and the Ferrari come back to earth at
the Flügplatz. 'A magic place, it was really eerie
because you could hear the cars from a long
way away and then they would flash into view
over the crest, and be gone in a split-second.
That must have been a Saturday morning
picture. You wouldn't go and shoot out there
during the race because it would be impossible
to get back to the pits for the finish.'

ACTION

Above: Monaco Grand Prix, Monte Carlo, 1969. The wide-angle lens dramatises the Lotus 49B-Cosworth V8 of Graham Hill *(top)* and Chris Amon's Ferrari 312/69 V12 as they negotiate the Station Hairpin. 'A relatively slow corner: it was a nice easy shot, but it always produced good results.'

ACTION

Above: Spanish Grand Prix, Montjuich Park,
Barcelona, 1969. Bruce McLaren *(top)* takes his
McLaren M7C to second place with the sunlight
dappling through the trees. Jochen Rindt
(above) fared less well. Soon after this picture
was taken, the rear aerofoil collapsed on his
Lotus 49B, pitching him into the Armco. He was
lucky to escape with relatively minor injuries.

ACTION

Dutch Grand Prix, Zandvoort, 1970. It was only
when he got his hands on a Lotus 72 that
Jochen Rindt could finally demonstrate his
talent consistently. 'This photo is a perfect one
to show the style of Rindt and the wonderful
lines of the 72.'

Race of Champions, Brands Hatch, 1970. *Trio at the Top* was the title of a contemporary book which chronicled the careers of Bruce McLaren, Denny Hulme and Chris Amon and it serves as an apt caption for this picture. The three Kiwis climb to the summit at Druids, with Amon's March 701 providing the meat in the McLaren sandwich.

ACTION

Three photos showing Jackie Stewart at work in Ken Tyrrell's cars.

Left: German Grand Prix, Nürburgring, 1971. The Scot entering the Karussell on his way to winning the race. 'You could see the rear-view mirrors shaking like crazy as the car bumped its way round the concrete.'

Below left: Austrian Grand Prix, Österreichring, 1972. 'A classic example of over- and understeer as Jackie's Tyrrell 005 leads Emerson Fittipaldi's JPS Lotus 72 through the Bosch Kurve. They are aiming the car right at you and going flat chat. Very brave men.'

Right: Monaco Grand Prix, Monte Carlo, 1971. 'This picture of Jackie was quite arty, with the huge spotlights and the mouth of the tunnel framing the car. But I was really working in the tunnel because it was the only place to stay dry during first practice when a torrential rainstorm swept the circuit.

'Monaco is always thought of as a sunny place but quite regularly over the years at least one day of the meeting has been affected by bad weather.'

ACTION

Left: The whistling Lotus 56B turbine car driven by Emerson Fittipaldi in the 1971 Race of Champions at Brands Hatch. 'They just used to whoosh past and were pretty bland. I don't think the drivers had the same sort of control as with the normal cars.'

Below: Belgian Grand Prix, Nivelles, 1972. 'There was no comparison between this place and Spa, but you could get some quite exciting pictures such as this one of the Ferrari 312B2s of Clay Regazzoni and Jacky Ickx, who is really working hard to stay with his team-mate.'

Right: French Grand Prix, Clermont-Ferrand, 1972. Emerson Fittipaldi races his JPS-liveried Lotus 72D towards second place in the race. 'A nice safe place to shoot the cars from high up on a bank.

'In sunny conditions such as these, the car photographed very well, but in dull weather it rather merged into the track. In the flesh it looked sensational at the time and very glamorous compared with the other cars. There are people who don't follow motor racing closely who think JPS are still involved, so strong was the branding.'

Race of Champions, Brands Hatch, 1972. Ronnie Peterson leaves his braking as late as possible in his March 721X and locks a wheel on the way into Druids Bend. 'That car was pretty awful and here it was a pig to drive, understeering into the corner and oversteering out of it. But Ronnie plugged away to the finish, though it must have been very disheartening for him to be so far off the pace.'

Monaco Grand Prix, Monte Carlo, 1974. 'It's the opening lap and side by side coming up the hill after the leaders are Denny Hulme (McLaren M23-Ford) and Jean-Pierre Beltoise (BRM). Their wheels are just about to interlock and a crash was inevitable. Nowadays they come up in single file, but then you tended to get the cars bunching, which made the pictures a lot more interesting and the racing more exciting!'

Above: Japanese Grand Prix, Fuji, 1976.
This was the first time a World Championship race had been held in Japan and of course all the interest was in the battle for the title between Hunt and Lauda. The race was run in torrential rain and this photo shows Patrick Depailler in the Tyrrell P34 six-wheeler ahead of Tom Pryce in the Shadow DN5B.

'I thought the Tyrrell was a strange-looking car, but on the right track and under the right conditions it could be very effective. At one time they fitted clear perspex windows on either side of the cockpit so that the fans could see the drivers at work. I thought that was great.'

ACTION

Above: Canadian Grand Prix, Mosport Park, 1976. Mario Andretti applies a touch of opposite lock at about 130 mph in the Lotus 77-Cosworth V8.

Left: French Grand Prix, Dijon, 1977. Niki Lauda's Ferrari 312T2 leads Ronnie Peterson in the Tyrrell P34-Cosworth. 'I like this picture because it's so clean and uncluttered, just the cloudless sky providing the backdrop.'

ACTION

United States Grand Prix West, Long Beach, 1977. Niki Lauda's Ferrari 312T2, which took second place in the race, scrambles around the tricky California street circuit. 'For a picture like this I used to shoot on sound, really. You could hear the car behind the building but you had very little warning before it appeared around the corner, so you focused on the spot where you wanted to capture the image. The trick was to decide who it was and whether you needed a shot of that particular driver or car!'

ACTION

Swedish Grand Prix, Anderstorp, 1978. Gilles
Villeneuve every whichway and loose.
'Jenks [the late Denis Jenkinson] thought he
was magnificent, a real racer; I thought he was
a bit wild. There's a few people who agree with
me. I watched him at every circuit. Lauda, for
instance, would go quicker and quicker on a
corner until he got it perfect; Villeneuve would
go quicker and quicker and just spin off. He
never realised the car's limits, which, perhaps,
was both his greatest strength and his greatest
weakness.'

ACTION

Top: French Grand Prix, Paul Ricard, 1978. John Watson in the Brabham BT46-Alfa flat-12 leads Alan Jones in the Williams FW06-Cosworth. The Australian is out of shape but nowhere near as much as Villeneuve in the background, who is experiencing a typically lurid moment of oversteer into the corner.

Above: French Grand Prix, Dijon, 1979. This was one of Grand Prix racing's most famous dices when Villeneuve and René Arnoux spent the final lap and a half of the race banging wheels with each other in the battle for second place.

'On the TV the viewer sees everything, with the help of replays and slow-motion, and this incident was very exciting. Of course when you are out on the circuit photographing the race you really don't have much idea of the general race pattern. Having mapped out which positions you are going to work from during the race, you just go from A to B taking your pictures. Maybe if you can see something like a driver making a dummy pass a couple of times at a certain spot you'll stay on because you know that's where it's likely to happen and you might get the overtaking manoeuvre.'

ACTION

Left: United States Grand Prix West, Long Beach, 1980. A typically aggressive action shot of Alan Jones in the Williams FW07-Cosworth. Although he became World Champion that season, he didn't win this particular race, being pushed out while lapping a back-marker. 'More than any other driver of that era, Jones always maximised the potential of his car. His driving style was probably best suited to those "ground-effect" cars.'

Above: French Grand Prix, Paul Ricard, 1982. Elio de Angelis gets the maximum from his tyres in his Lotus 91-Cosworth V8. 'On the last corner before the pits, the cars used to run up the kerbing here and you could hear a rumbling noise from the tyres as they did so.'

Left: British Grand Prix, Silverstone, 1981. John Watson wins the British Grand Prix in his John Barnard-designed McLaren MP4-Cosworth. 'This was a bit of a lucky win for "Wattie" because Arnoux's Renault hit trouble close to the end of the race. But it was the first victory for McLaren under the stewardship of Ron Dennis, and, after a couple of years in the doldrums, the team really started to take off.'

ACTION

South African Grand Prix, Kyalami, 1983.
Nelson Piquet getting crossed up in his
Brabham BT52B-BMW. It was the last race of
an exciting year, and he clinched the drivers'
championship after Prost retired his Renault.
'This season saw the introduction of
flat-bottomed cars, which were nimbler and
easier to drive, and the widespread adoption of
mid-race refuelling tactics, pioneered by
Brabham the previous year.'

ACTION

Below: United States Grand Prix West, Long Beach, 1983. Arnoux's Ferrari squats down on its front suspension after crashing over one of the street course's notorious bumps. 'This particular hazard was removed overnight, which must have been a relief for the drivers, but it was not half as exciting for the photographers.'

Bottom: European Grand Prix, Brands Hatch, 1983. The Ferrari of Arnoux and the Renault of Cheever interlock wheels as they round Druids. 'I don't know whether this is Eddie Cheever trying something incredibly brave or René Arnoux being stupid. Or vice-versa. You would never see two cars like that today.'

Left: Monaco Grand Prix, Monte Carlo, 1984. Nigel Mansell leading the most prestigious race of them all. Unfortunately it ended in tears for Nigel when he put the car into the barriers. 'At this stage in his career it looked as though he was never going to win a Grand Prix. But he made his detractors eat their words.'

Below: Belgian Grand Prix, Spa-Francorchamps, 1985. 'When it rains at Spa (and it invariably does sometime during the weekend), you get very, very wet. It's hard to keep the cameras dry and you seem to spend most of the time slipping around on the muddy banks at the side of the track. No matter, one has to keep on working – just like Keke Rosberg in his Williams FW10-Honda.'

Left: Brazilian Grand Prix, Jacarepaguá, 1985. Michele Alboreto on his way to second place in the Ferrari 156/85 V6. 'This shot shows how far forward the drivers were positioned in the cars of this period. Not much in the way of protection at the front for their legs and feet – nor at the sides for that matter.'

Left: German Grand Prix, Hockenheim, 1986. Having run out of fuel within sight of the chequered flag, Alain Prost heroically pushes his McLaren MP4/2C towards the finish line. He eventually abandoned the unequal struggle and settled for sixth place. 'Man and machine not as nature intended.'

Below: Monaco Grand Prix, Monte Carlo, 1988. Gerhard Berger working the wheel of his Ferrari around Loews. 'Compare this photo to the ones taken at La Source at the beginning of the chapter and see how much more enclosed in the car the driver has become.'

Left: British Grand Prix, Brands Hatch, 1986. Nigel Mansell wins on his home patch in his Williams FW11-Honda, delighting the fans again after his victory in the European Grand Prix only a few months earlier. 'This was the last time a Grand Prix was held at Brands, which is a real shame. It was such a great circuit to photograph at, with its elevation changes and interesting corners – in contrast with the flat and rather featureless expanses of Silverstone, which I've never much cared for.'

ACTION

Above: Monaco Grand Prix, Monte Carlo, 1992. 'Senna won this race six times – a master at work.'

Above right: Brazilian Grand Prix, Interlagos, 1992. Senna, at the wheel of the McLaren MP4/7A-Honda, leads the new rising star Michael Schumacher in the Benetton B191B-Ford. Tailing the pair are Jean Alesi's Ferrari F92A and the second Benetton of Martin Brundle. 'Coming up with interesting group shots of cars like this gets harder and harder as they now tend to become spread out very quickly after a race gets under way.'

ACTION

Left: Italian Grand Prix, Monza, 1991. Nelson Piquet gets it all wrong at the first chicane in his Benetton B191-Ford. 'This is always a good spot for a dramatic picture. Photographing the start from here is almost obligatory nowadays as there is invariably an incident of some kind.'

Below: Canadian Grand Prix, Montreal, 1996. David Coulthard wrestling the McLaren MP4/11-Mercedes around the hairpin. 'It's now so difficult to shoot here as you have to poke your lenses through small holes in the safety fence. In addition you have security people who seem to deliberately stand in your way and make life difficult.'

Left: Monaco Grand Prix, Monte Carlo, 1993. Alain Prost screams through the tunnel in his Williams FW15C-Renault. The Frenchman led the race from pole but was penalised with a stop–go penalty for a jumped start. 'The tunnel is much better lit these days, with the fluorescent lighting. Note the triple layer of Armco which now dwarfs the cars around the circuit. The drivers must see nothing but Armco nowadays.'

ACTION

Right: Monaco Grand Prix, Monte Carlo, 1996. Jacques Villeneuve, then Formula 1's 'new kid on the block', with the Williams FW18. He crashed out of this race, but quickly showed his talent by establishing himself as Michael Schumacher's biggest rival.

Below: Villeneuve pressurises the German's Ferrari in the Hungarian Grand Prix later that season. 'The Hungaroring is one of the best tracks to shoot at nowadays. The weather is usually hot and dry and the light is wonderful.'

Australian Grand Prix, Melbourne, 1998. A new
breed of Formula 1 car and a new era in motor
racing as the McLaren-Mercedes-Bridgestone
partnership seems poised to displace Williams
from their long-held position of dominance.
This event was particularly contentious due to a
pre-race agreement between drivers Mika
Häkkinen *(above)* and David Coulthard that the
leader through the first corner should take the
win. 'The FIA have subsequently announced
they will crack down on this sort of practice, but
in reality how can you stop it?'

ACTION

chapter 6
drama, triumph and tragedy

Drama and Nigel Mansell were never far apart throughout the Englishman's career. 'Nigel could never resist finding some minor problem or other which he heroically had to overcome in order to prevail in the end. That said, he was easily one of the most exciting drivers I have ever seen.'

Three very different moods at the Monaco Grand Prix.

Left: The 1966 race brings joy for Jackie Stewart as he takes the win for BRM. Louis Chiron gives a typically flamboyant flourish with the chequered flag. 'Chiron was unreal. He just used to run into the road almost in front of the cars at the finish – how he wasn't killed I'll never know.'

Above: Lorenzo Bandini pays the ultimate price in 1967 after crashing at the harbour chicane in his Ferrari. Badly burned, the Italian clung to life for three days before succumbing to his injuries.

'When something like this happens there is a terrible silence. I was shooting down from opposite Rosie's Bar and couldn't see that much because of the trees but I knew something awful had happened. Even though there were marshals and the like on the track the race carried on . . .'

Left: Embarrassment for Jack Brabham. The normally unflappable Australian limps across the line into second place after being pressurised into a last-corner shunt by Jochen Rindt's late charge, which won him the 1970 race. 'The pits in the background were super-dangerous. You can see all those people standing in the pit area with no protection, nothing between them and the track.'

DRAMA, TRIUMPH & TRAGEDY

Even the greatest of drivers have the occasional embarrassing moments and here are two photos to prove it.

Left: Jim Clark spins into the straw bales during practice for the 1967 Monaco Grand Prix. This was Diana Burnett's first Grand Prix armed with a camera and under instructions from Nigel. 'I thought this would be a nice easy place for her to stand among the straw bales, where she would be perfectly safe. I told her, "If anything happens, take a picture." She must have been unfazed by the Lotus spinning towards her, because click-click-click and her first professional motor racing picture was in the bag.'

Above: Jackie Stewart goes cross-country combine harvesting after spinning out at Stowe Corner during the 1973 British Grand Prix. 'I remember Jackie was very angry with a couple of photographers who were almost mowed down by his Tyrrell. Thankfully he narrowly avoided them.'

DRAMA, TRIUMPH & TRAGEDY

Nothing beats winning and the joy of both the driver and his team are captured in these three photos.

Left: Brabham mechanics are on the track as they applaud Carlos Reutemann's win in the 1975 German Grand Prix. 'The figures in the foreground make it a much more interesting photo than just the car crossing the line. Now, of course, personnel on the track are *verboten*.'

Right: James Hunt scores a fairy-tale win for Hesketh in the 1975 Dutch Grand Prix. 'This was James's first Grand Prix win and I love the way his arms are aloft out of the cockpit as if about to embrace Lord Hesketh (in the white shirt).'

Below right: An even greater moment for James in the 1976 Japanese Grand Prix, but he hasn't quite realised yet that he is the new World Champion. 'The McLaren team boss Teddy Mayer shows him three fingers indicating that his third place was enough to see him snatch the title from Niki Lauda by a single point.'

DRAMA, TRIUMPH & TRAGEDY

Above: The 1976 Monaco Grand Prix fell to
Niki Lauda in the Ferrari. During his victory
lap, the Austrian cruises down past the Hotel
Metropole to rapturous applause. 'A few of the
crowd are over the Armco; spectators would
never be allowed to watch the race from such a
dangerous spot as this now.'

DRAMA, TRIUMPH & TRAGEDY

First-lap drama at the British Grand Prix.

Left: Complete and utter mayhem in the 1973 race as Jody Scheckter spears his McLaren into the pit wall and causes a chain reaction in the pack behind. Stewart, unawares, leads into Copse. 'Unfortunately this was the only shot I got of this accident. I remember there were cars all over the place and it took quite a while before the race could be restarted.'

Below: Forward to Brands Hatch in 1976 and James Hunt in the McLaren *(right)* is the innocent victim of Clay Regazzoni's spinning Ferrari. Mario Andretti takes a quick look over to see the incident. A day of high drama ensued. Hunt was initially excluded from the restart because, with his car damaged, he had failed to complete the opening lap, but pressure from the 77,000 crowd forced the organisers into a rethink and the local hero was back in the race in his repaired car. In true Hollywood style, Hunt went on to win from arch-rival Lauda, but nearly two months later he was disqualified on appeal.

Left: French Grand Prix, Rouen, 1968. A ball of flame engulfs the crashed Honda of Jo Schlesser. The enormously popular Frenchman had longed for the chance to drive a pukka Formula 1 car and at the age of 40 he was invited to race the experimental air-cooled Honda RA302 in his home Grand Prix. It ended in disaster on lap three when the engine cut out and he crashed at high speed into an earth bank.

'I was walking back to the pits. Just prior to that I had heard the engine cutting in and out and I presumed he had just lost it. I didn't realise the poor guy was still in the car. After the race in the paddock there were French journalists in tears.'

Left: Dutch Grand Prix, Zandvoort, 1973. A pall of smoke drifts over the circuit as Niki Lauda's BRM emerges. Behind lies Roger Williamson, trapped in his overturned car. 'David Purley tried in vain to help, but everyone else, as was the norm in those days, just raced on. Even if I had been at the spot I wouldn't have wanted close-up pictures of the accident.'

Above: Italian Grand Prix, Monza, 1978. The aftermath of the accident that claimed the life of Ronnie Peterson. The stricken Swede lies in the centre of the picture being given first aid while the other drivers wander about among the abandoned cars.

'I remember hearing that he had been taken to hospital but that his life was not in danger. It was only when I arrived home that Di told me that complications had set in and he had died. I was terribly sad; it was a dreadful blow. It was one of the times you really feel, "What's the point of this?"'

DRAMA, TRIUMPH & TRAGEDY

Left: Austrian Grand Prix, Österreichring, 1975. Mark Donohue in the Penske just seconds from disaster, with his left-front tyre beginning to deflate. The car left the track and careered into the catch fencing, which just launched it over the Armco into an area where two unfortunate marshals were sitting.

'I remember rushing over to the scene and there was this alsatian dog just whimpering and one of the marshals was split right open. He later died. They got Donohue out and he was sitting on the track talking quite lucidly to the first-aid crew. He must have hit his helmet on some tubular steel scaffolding, because he later collapsed on the way to hospital and, despite brain surgery, died the following Tuesday.'

Above: South African Grand Prix, Kyalami, 1977. The tangled wreckage to the left is all that remains of the Shadow of Tom Pryce. The poor Welshman was involved in a bizarre accident when a marshal ran across the track with a fire extinguisher and was hit by the Shadow. The marshal was killed instantly, as was Pryce, struck in the face by the heavy extinguisher. The car continued at unabated speed down the track and clipped the back of Laffite's Ligier before smashing into the fencing at Crowthorne Corner.

'The incident between Pryce and the marshal happened in a dip way back down the straight, and at first we didn't realise that anything was wrong. It was only when the car failed to brake that we knew it was out of control.'

DRAMA, TRIUMPH & TRAGEDY

115

Left: Race of Champions, Brands Hatch, 1973. John Watson crashed his new Brabham BT42 at Stirlings Bend quite early in the race.
'He was trapped for some time while the rescue crew worked to cut him free and was in quite a bit of pain because of a broken leg. But he seemed to want to talk. I said, "I'm going to take a couple of shots, John." And he replied, "Yes, OK – go ahead." '

Top: Australian Grand Prix, Adelaide, 1986. Nigel Mansell struggles to bring his car to a halt after suffering a tyre burst on the straight, leaving his World Championship dream in tatters. Di got this shot. 'That's all I could see from the angle I was shooting.' Philippe Alliot turns his Ligier into the corner unaware just how close he is to being collected by the Williams.

Above: Dutch Grand Prix, Zandvoort, 1979. Another famous incident as Gilles Villeneuve attempts to make it back to the pits to replace a punctured tyre, but has only succeeded in destroying his Ferrari's rear suspension. 'Situation normal for Gilles. There were grooves gouged in the track and bits hanging off all over the place. It was just ridiculous, it really was.'

DRAMA, TRIUMPH & TRAGEDY

German Grand Prix, Hockenheim, 1994. One of the most spectacular incidents of recent years was the blaze which engulfed Jos Verstappen while he was making a routine pit stop in the Benetton. Happily, no one was seriously injured but it could have been catastrophic. A salutary reminder that in the mega-dangerous world of Formula 1, the possibility of disaster is ever-present.

'Di was one of the designated photographers on the pit wall for this race, and we needed a photo of Verstappen in black and white for one of the many magazines we were working for, otherwise we would have been shooting in colour. The incident actually only lasted a few seconds and she got the whole sequence. If the shots had been in colour we could have earned a hundred times more than we did, but that's the way it goes.'

DRAMA, TRIUMPH & TRAGEDY

Black magic. Team Lotus may have been consigned to the history books but they figure large in the folklore of Grand Prix racing, having achieved 79 victories between 1958 and 1994. Their creative genius was founder Colin Chapman, who built a racing team that conquered the world and road cars that still thrill enthusiasts to this day.

Right: A familiar scene in the 1970s as Chapman greets yet another Lotus victory. 'You knew Colin was always going to do that – throw his cap in the air – but it still made for a good picture. Nowadays it's an image which everybody thinks of when you mention him.'

Above left: Portuguese Grand Prix, Estoril, 1985. Sheer joy all round as Ayrton Senna wins his first Grand Prix in the most appalling conditions. A jubilant Senna is welcomed home by wheel-men Clive and Kenny and team manager Peter Warr. Confirmation, if it was needed, that a truly stellar talent had arrived.

Left: Austrian Grand Prix, Österreichring, 1982. The raised arm of Elio de Angelis signals he has just beaten Keke Rosberg to the line in a thrilling finish. It was the quiet Italian's first Grand Prix win. 'One of the closest finishes I've ever seen: I knew if I stood at this angle I would get both cars, whichever made it to the line first.'

Because of their history Ferrari are still the foremost name in motor racing. Success and failure seem to go hand-in-hand for the Prancing Horse, as these three photos so vividly illustrate.

Left: Italian Grand Prix, Monza, 1975. 'It doesn't get any better than this. A Ferrari 1-2, Niki Lauda the new World Champion, and *tifosi* favourite Clay Regazzoni *(left)* the race winner.'

Above: San Marino Grand Prix, Imola, 1982. Gilles Villeneuve's face sums up his mood after team-mate Didier Pironi had disobeyed team orders to take a contentious win. 'Once you know the context, this picture needs no further explanation.'

Right: Those were the days, my friend. Di's photo of a contemplative Niki Lauda sums up Ferrari's sagging fortunes in the mid-Nineties. 'The arrival of Michael Schumacher has galvanised the team, and with Ross Brawn and Rory Byrne on board, they are now a force to be reckoned with.'

DRAMA, TRIUMPH & TRAGEDY

The last lap. San Marino Grand Prix, Imola, 1994. The Williams of Ayrton Senna enters the chicane and heads towards the start-finish line ahead of Michael Schumacher in the Benetton. 'This was the last picture I shot of Ayrton; only moments later he crashed fatally at Tamburello. Everyone was stunned. This accident, coming straight after Roland Ratzenberger's death on the Saturday, made it a nightmarish weekend. I count myself very fortunate to have a profession which is so enjoyable, but times like this leave you with little heart for it.'

DRAMA, TRIUMPH & TRAGEDY

The joy of winning.

Left: United States Grand Prix West, Long Beach, 1983. Victory was sweet for John Watson and he follows the time-honoured tradition of spraying the Moët.

Below: Hungarian Grand Prix, Hungaroring, 1986. The FIA were becoming concerned that trophies were getting so large and heavy that dignitaries would soon have difficulty presenting them to the drivers. At this race suitably modest mementoes were distributed. Nelson Piquet, ever the joker, sends up the situation, while Mansell *(right)* looks bored by it all. 'Unless Nigel was on the top step of the podium, he wasn't terribly interested.'

DRAMA, TRIUMPH & TRAGEDY

Left: Japanese Grand Prix, Suzuka, 1991. Gerhard Berger looks somewhat bewildered as he takes in his first win for McLaren. 'Having already secured the championship due to Mansell's early retirement in the race, Ayrton Senna *(left)* slowed on the last lap to allow his team-mate the win.'

Below: Belgian Grand Prix, Spa-Francorchamps, 1997. Michael Schumacher provided yet another of his brilliant wet-weather performances to destroy the opposition. 'Schumacher is a joy to photograph on the podium because he always has a big smile on his face and it makes such a difference. There was a time a few seasons ago when the drivers looked bored, they won so often. When Michael came along it was like a breath of fresh air.'

Left: Italian Grand Prix, Monza, 1994. Arms aloft, Damon Hill is once more the hero after his win.

Below: San Marino Grand Prix, Imola, 1997. Nowhere man: Damon abandons his Arrows, having run into the back of Shinji Nakano's Prost out of sheer frustration. 'Everybody loves drivers while they are winning, but when they start to slip down the grid – for whatever reason – the past is quickly forgotten and criticism begins.'

DRAMA, TRIUMPH & TRAGEDY

chapter 7
people

'Motor racing has always been a social sport. By that I mean that the competitors by and large mix with the press and the photographers. Of course it's not nearly so friendly these days but the stakes are high and the media scrums so large that the drivers need to escape to the privacy of their motorhomes to concentrate their thoughts on the next session of practice. Compared to most sports, the access we have is still marvellous.' This chapter goes behind the scenes of Grand Prix racing and the candid pictures give a flavour of the paddock and the off-track world of Formula 1.

Above: Niki Lauda is introduced to a koala bear at Adelaide in 1985. 'Niki's expression indicates he seems more frightened of the meeting with the marsupial than the everyday business of racing a Formula 1 car!'

PEOPLE

129

Left: 'I wish the McLaren I drove in 1978 had been half as good as this one.' James Hunt, then a TV commentator, looks over a new McLaren and gives team boss Ron Dennis his impressions.

Below: Sitting in the cockpit of one of his beautifully presented McLaren M23s before a demonstration run at the Goodwood Festival of Speed in 1995, Ron Dennis shares a joke with Martin Brundle, one of the team's regular drivers that season. The pressure is off and, for this weekend at least, Ron can relax and enjoy himself.

Letting the hands do the talking. Enzo Ferrari *(top)*, Mauro Forghieri *(above)* and Luca di Montezemolo *(right)* emphasise their points in typically Italian style.

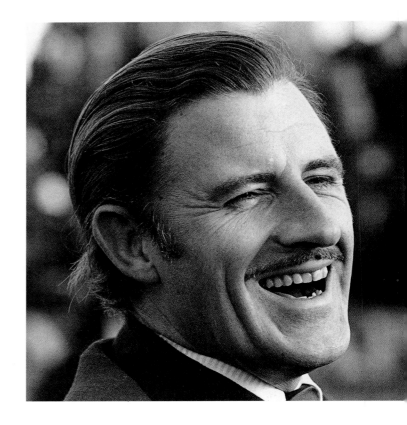

Above: Colin Chapman in 1982. 'The pressures of running Lotus must have been enormous. His death from a heart attack in December of that year came as a huge shock, but, in hindsight, this picture shows the stress he must have endured in that last period of his life.'

Above right: By complete contrast, Graham Hill captured in carefree mood, looking relaxed and full of fun. This shot was taken before the London–Sydney marathon in 1968.

Right: French Grand Prix, Clermont-Ferrand, 1969. No motorhomes or hospitality suites here, thank you. Just find a spare patch of ground by a fence and let the meeting begin. The Lotus quartet of Jochen Rindt, Colin Chapman, Graham Hill and John Miles sit in the paddock discussing practice. 'There were so few photographers at this race that you could easily take photos like this as long as you weren't too intrusive and seen to be listening in on private conversations.'

PEOPLE

Above: The launch of the Lotus 72 in 1970. 'In those days, just a small number of journalists and photographers would cover the launch of a new racing car. There were probably fewer than 50 people at Hethel when I took this shot. Colin *(right)* casually showed the group around the car and we were allowed to shoot any detail pictures we wanted. After about 20 minutes or so, Jochen Rindt got into the car and drove out onto the test track so we could get some action shots. It was as simple and unpretentious as that.'

PEOPLE

Such has been the dominance of Williams Grand Prix Engineering over the past decade that it is easy to forget the years of struggle that Frank Williams spent establishing himself in Formula 1.

Left: He chats with his first driver, Piers Courage, at Zandvoort in 1969. A year later at the same track Courage was killed at the wheel of Frank's car and Williams lost not only a fine driver but a close friend.

Below left: Crucial to the Williams team's subsequent success has been Patrick Head, whose engineering talents helped provide a succession of championship-winning cars. This picture was taken at Detroit in 1986 as he confers with Nigel Mansell. 'Patrick has always been kind and considerate towards us; he really is a very nice person.'

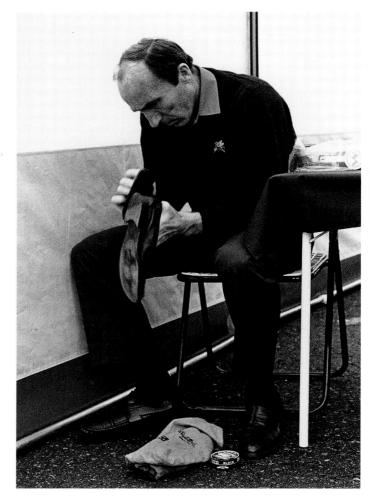

Above: 'Super Rat'. 'With this profile, it could only be Niki.'

Right: David Thieme was on the scene for a while as a major sponsor of the Lotus team when it ran in Essex Petroleum colours. 'Both a flamboyant and a mysterious figure. This picture sums up the latter persona.'

Below: James in his element in Rio. 'He was always at home among the pretty girls and enjoyed the social aspect that is part and parcel of Formula 1.'

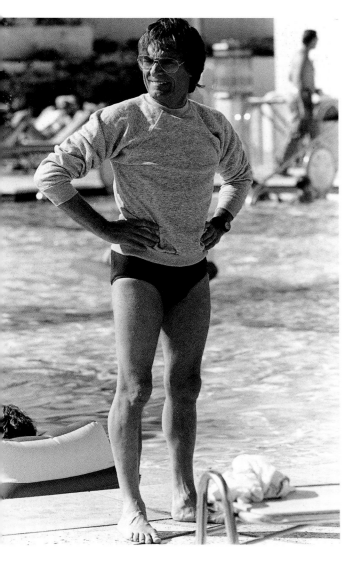

Top left: The end of another long, hard season and Bernie Ecclestone allows himself time to enjoy the sunshine by the pool. Las Vegas, 1982.

Top: 'A word in your ear.' For a while Ecclestone and Jean-Marie Balestre were locked in conflict during the FISA–FOCA 'war'.

Above: 'Bernie holds all the cards, as Balestre eventually found out.'

Left: The late Nineties and still calling the shots. 'He's a man of his word. If Bernie promises to do something, he will. Everybody who makes a living out of Formula 1 has reason to be grateful for the work Bernie has done over the years. He has done a superb job packaging Grand Prix racing and we have all benefited from his efforts.'

PEOPLE

Right: Samba time in Brazil at a particularly memorable Elf party. 'Carnival girls were brought in to do a floor show and I was trying to dance with the girl in the centre and take a photo simultaneously. It was a bit unnerving as everything seemed to be moving in different directions at the same time!'

Below: 'This was another Elf party, this time one with a South Sea Island theme at Paul Ricard in 1975. I shot this picture of Michèle Depailler, Pam Scheckter and Bette Hill which was then published in a magazine. Pam later came up to me and said, "Snowdon, that party picture you took is showing my panties!" Thereafter whenever we saw each other I was given the V-sign by Pam, but as you can see *(below right)* it was all very good natured. She was a lovely lady.'

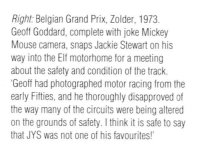

Right: Belgian Grand Prix, Zolder, 1973. Geoff Goddard, complete with joke Mickey Mouse camera, snaps Jackie Stewart on his way into the Elf motorhome for a meeting about the safety and condition of the track. 'Geoff had photographed motor racing from the early Fifties, and he thoroughly disapproved of the way many of the circuits were being altered on the grounds of safety. I think it is safe to say that JYS was not one of his favourites!'

PEOPLE

Three occasional photographers hunting pictures.

Above: Leo Sayer. 'I shot this picture in South Africa, and at the time I didn't know who he was. We got talking, and when he found out I was Nigel Snowdon and the shot was for *Autocourse*, he was really chuffed, because he is a big fan of my work and the book. He later signed this print thanking us for making him famous!'

Top right: Cameras at five paces. 'Jochen Mass borrowed this little camera of mine and became the photographer as well as the subject.'

Above right: The great Denis Jenkinson, known to all as 'Jenks', and his Rollei. 'I don't think he approved of 35 mm cameras. He was always criticising me for being too "arty". I once did a road test with him and I shot a Porsche with coloured filters to make the sky interesting. After seeing it he came to me and said, "When I want someone to photograph the End of the World, I'll come and see you first."'

Right: Alan Jones on one of his more friendly days!

Left: Stefan Bellof and Manfred Winkelhock larking about in the pits. 'Now it makes a very sad picture as they were both killed within months of each other racing sports cars.'

Below: Stefan Johansson and Michele Alboreto were great team-mates at Ferrari. 'Michele takes time at the end of a photocall to have a bit of fun for the cameras.'

Left: Wizards of Oz: 'Alan Jones and Clive James both reached the top of their chosen professions without losing their typically Australian no-nonsense and down-to-earth approach.'

PEOPLE

Left: Bloodied but unbowed, Innes Ireland after an attempted mugging in Rio de Janeiro, 1986. 'They tried to steal his Ferrari watch, but they didn't realise what they were taking on. According to Innes, one of the attackers left with a very high-pitched voice!'

Above: The end of the road. Renault pulled out of Formula 1 in 1985 and have never returned as a fully fledged constructor. Since 1989 they have concentrated on the supply of engines which have powered Williams (five times) and Benetton (once) to the constructors' championship on six occasions. 'The mechanic was happy to sit there with the signs behind him. It was a bit of a set-up shot but quite effective nevertheless.'

Left: John Watswrong: 'McLaren's fortunes were at a low ebb in 1979, but perhaps the mechanics thought "Wattie" protested too much about the car's shortcomings. Teddy Mayer (centre) looks as impassive and unimpressed as ever.'

PEOPLE

Right: On the long-haul flight to North America in 1973, Helen Stewart and François Cevert grab some sleep. Tragically, the young Frenchman was to lose his life in a practice accident at Watkins Glen.

'I was just walking down the aisle and grabbed this picture. He was obviously a talented driver who benefited greatly from working with Ken Tyrrell. Sadly he never had the chance to step from Jackie's shadow and prove his championship potential.'

Below: French Grand Prix, Magny-Cours, 1997. Running your own team is hard work and the chairman of Stewart Grand Prix helps to sweep out the flooded pit during practice. 'Jackie always likes to be busy; he's still a real bundle of energy and there is nothing he won't turn his hand to.'

Below right: When Stewart Grand Prix was just a dream? Austrian Grand Prix, Österreichring, 1983. Dad has seen it all before, but a young Paul watches intently as the cars go by. 'This was just an attractive shot at the time, but of course now the pic has a nice tag to it.'

Opposite; clockwise from top left: On his way to greatness: a youthful Michael Schumacher, photographed in 1992. 'Michael is without doubt the most professional driver I have ever photographed. He is intelligent, immaculate and aware of his responsibilities – and unlike some other drivers today he doesn't make life more difficult for us photographers than it has to be.'

With Benetton's fortunes fading in 1997, team boss Flavio Briatore ponders his future. 'He was a real character and he loved to be photographed. He really revelled in his time in Formula 1 with its jet-setting lifestyle.'

If you are an Englishman, wherever you are in the world, nothing beats a good cup of tea. Damon Hill partakes of said refreshment.

Since coming into Formula 1 in 1991 team owner Eddie Jordan has encountered his fair share of disappointments but he has managed to retain his sense of fun.

Ross Brawn searches for solutions to the problems presented by Ferrari's quest for that elusive World Championship.

Ken Tyrrell was the last surviving link with
Nigel's early days as a Grand Prix
photographer. 'I was doing a shoot with Ken
and Norah at their home, and as I was finishing
Ken said, "I must do the lawn." At the time it
was rumoured that he was going to get Honda
engines, and this was a good, topical, fun
picture. Fun is something that I always
associate with Ken; his enthusiasm for all
kinds of sport is incredible.'

PEOPLE

chapter 8
sporting types

Grand Prix drivers are necessarily competitive individuals, and this extends to other sports, even if they are not pursued with quite the same dedication. This light-hearted chapter catches the superstars off-duty but still concentrating intently as they engage in various sporting pursuits.

Right: David Coulthard looks happy with this shot at a charity golf match. 'I think David will be the first to admit that he should still stick with his day job!'

Above: 'Graham Hill pursued a game of table tennis with the same vigour as his racing. He was always a competitor.'

Right: Larry Perkins goes weight training with Seventies state-of-the-art equipment. 'Larry never got the breaks in F1, but he has since done really well in Australia both as a racer and as an engineer.'

Below right: Anyone for tennis? Ronnie Peterson goes for the net. 'Ronnie wasn't the greatest of natural athletes. There wasn't a lot you could say about his tennis style because he didn't have any, but he was always willing to join in the activities and enjoy himself.

'These Kyalami tennis tournaments were always a delight and Mario Andretti, though looking more competitive than Ronnie, was another who played in the spirit of fun that was intended.'

Cricket is a game that holds hidden mysteries for the uninitiated and a Grand Prix cricket team reflecting the cosmopolitan make-up of the starting grid was bound to provide huge entertainment. For a number of years, on the day following the British Grand Prix, the star drivers of the time duly donned the whites for a charity event.

Above: This motley crew comes from the 1974 season and comprises: *Back (l to r):* Ken Tyrrell, John Watson, Guy Edwards, Mike Hailwood, James Hunt, Graham Hill, Patrick Depailler, Peter Gethin, David Purley and Clay Regazzoni; *Front (l to r):* Jody Scheckter, Derek Bell, Niki Lauda, Emerson Fittipaldi, Ronnie Peterson, Jochen Mass and Denny Hulme.

'These matches were great fun. Mike Hailwood had a bottle of wine positioned out on the boundary while he was fielding, and invited Di and me for a drink. It was hilarious to see the likes of Emerson Fittipaldi *(left)* attempt to master the art of batting.'

SPORTING TYPES

There's golf and there's golf. Nigel Mansell was so accomplished that he was deemed good enough to play as an amateur in the Australian Open *(left)*.

Johnny Herbert *(below left)* and Mika Häkkinen *(below)* are just happy to scratch around the course in less pressured circumstances at a charity match.

Right: Damon Hill takes up the challenge of archery. It is to be hoped that his acquaintance with this type of arrows proved more satisfactory than his 1997 season with Tom Walkinshaw's team.

Top left: Ayrton Senna was fascinated by radio-controlled model cars and aeroplanes. 'This shot was taken at Brands Hatch during a break in proceedings at the 1986 British Grand Prix.'

Above: Michael Schumacher and his wife Corinna join forces at table football.

Left: Which one's mine? The Japanese commentator's nightmare, Brundle and Blundell, deep in concentration as they compete at slot-car racing.

SPORTING TYPES

Grand Prix United. This is the 1984 squad in Canada assembled to take on the cream of journalistic talent. Suffice it to say this group of speed merchants won. *Back (l to r):* Stefan Bellof, Riccardo Patrese, Nigel Mansell, Andrea de Cesaris, Johnny Cecotto, Michele Alboreto, Eddie Cheever and Manfred Winkelhock. *Front (l to r):* Elio de Angelis, Philippe Alliot, Derek Warwick and Ayrton Senna.

SPORTING TYPES

chapter 9
around the world

Although Grand Prix racing is seen as the pinnacle of motor sport, there are many other categories of racing that have been the subject of Nigel's lenses. This final chapter spotlights some interesting and offbeat photos taken down the years, not necessarily in Formula 1.

Above: Ronnie Peterson sits quietly in his BMW turbo before taking Nigel onto the Brands Hatch circuit for a demonstration. 'Ronnie said, "Come on, I'll take you out for a few laps." I was taking photos as we went round, but soon put down my camera and just watched him at work. It was fascinating to see the movements of his hands on the wheel and his feet dancing on the pedals. I'm sure that if I had looked up I would have been scared half to death!'

The Tasman series in the 1960s provided fans in Australia and New Zealand with the opportunity to see the Grand Prix stars of the day in slightly modified Formula 1 cars. For the drivers, it was a chance to soak up the sun and enjoy some racing before returning to Europe for the World Championship campaign.

Left: Denny Hulme and Goodyear's Barry Griffin lift a Repco engine into the back of the Brabham. 'Denny was a very good engineer as well as a terrific driver.'

Above: Jackie Stewart takes the chance to demonstrate his versatility, as his dedication of the print suggests. 'Minimal numbers of team personnel were employed on a series such as this and the drivers had to muck in and lend a hand, as seen in the picture *(left)* of Jim Clark changing a wheel during practice.'

Above: Jackie Stewart at Lakeside in the BRM. 'The lack of barriers around parts of the track gave me the opportunity to take photos like this one, which has just three elements: sky, car and grass verge.'

Right: Jack Brabham, Jackie Stewart and Jim Clark find time for a chat at Sandown Park. 'In this day and age you would never get the likes of Schumacher, Hill and Villeneuve standing casually around in the paddock engaged in conversation. They have to be brought together by PR people for a photo opportunity.'

AROUND THE WORLD

Putting on a show. Denny Hulme, all crossed up in his Brabham at the Warwick Farm Esses in 1967. 'He used to pass me every time like this – virtually sideways. Magic!'

The Sports Car World Championship was much more important in the scheme of things in the late Sixties and early Seventies. The major players such as Ford, Ferrari and Porsche invested huge sums of money in their attempts to achieve success. Top Grand Prix drivers of the day could earn substantial sums of money by racing these cars when not on Formula 1 duty.

Above: The old Spa circuit at Stavelot makes a brooding study as a prototype chases a much slower GT car. 'When they changed the circuit it lost much of its magic for me.'

Left: Nigel won the Guild of Motoring Writers' first-ever Gwen Salmon Award with this photo of the turbine-engined Howmet TX driven by Dick Thompson in the 1968 BOAC 500 race at Brands Hatch.

AROUND THE WORLD

Left: Up yours. 'I worked on the film *Le Mans* which starred Steve McQueen. Being American, he gesticulated with the single finger until I told him about the V-sign which was used in Europe. Thereafter, whenever he saw me, he used to greet me with the said V, and also used it at the end of the film.'

Below: Two Porsche 917s head into Tertre Rouge during the 1970 race. 'This was a great place to shoot, and it sums up the magic of Le Mans. Even today, it still has a special atmosphere.'

Left: Graham Hill getting very sideways in a Lotus-Cortina. 'The cliché about Graham was that he wasn't a natural driver, but one that worked extremely hard to reach the top. That may be so, but I can tell you he was incredibly fast in anything he drove.'

Right: Support your local sheriff. United States Grand Prix, Watkins Glen, 1974. Clay Regazzoni's abandoned Ferrari is guarded by one of America's finest.

Right: Caesars Palace Grand Prix, Las Vegas, 1981. 'I fought the law and the law won.' Journalist Mike Doodson shows his handcuffed wrists after an altercation with the local police. 'Mike wanted to go somewhere out on the circuit and the security men denied him access despite his credentials. Before he knew it, he was under arrest. Fortunately, the situation was eventually defused and Mike was free to pursue his journalistic duties.'

Left: British Grand Prix, Brands Hatch, 1976. 'No, sir, you cannot go out and practise.' 'Quite how this oddball and his tricycle made it onto the pit lane alongside James Hunt's McLaren it's hard to imagine.'

'Don't cry for me, Argentina.'

'The Girl from Ipanema.'